Hands-On Science Fun

How to Make a

Pom-Pom FLYER

A 4D Book

by Barbara Alpert

PEBBLE

a capstone imprint

Pebble Plus is published by Capstone Press,
1710 Roe Crest Drive, North Mankato, Minnesota 56003
www.mycapstone.com

Library of Congress Cataloging-in-Publication Data
is available on the Library of Congress website.

ISBN 978-1-9771-0224-9 (library binding)
ISBN 978-1-9771-0515-8 (paperback)
ISBN 978-1-9771-0228-7 (ebook pdf)

Editorial Credits
Carrie Braulick Sheely, editor; Sarah Bennett, designer;
Marcy Morin, scheduler and project producer;
Sarah Schuette, photo stylist and project producer;
Katy LaVigne, production specialist

Photo Credits
All photographs by Capstone Studio/Karon Dubke except for:
Shutterstock/Suriya KK, cover (arrows)

Note to Parents and Teachers

The Hands-On Science Fun set supports national science standards related to physical science. This book describes and illustrates making a pom-pom flyer. The images support early readers in understanding the text. The repetition of words and phrases helps early readers learn new words. This book also introduces early readers to subject-specific vocabulary words, which are defined in the Glossary section. Early readers may need assistance to read some words and to use the Table of Contents, Glossary, Read More, Internet Sites, Critical Thinking Questions, and Index sections of the book.

1. Ask an adult to download the app.

   Capstone 4D
   Education

2. Scan the pages with the star.

3. Enjoy your cool stuff!

—— OR ——

Use this password at capstone4D.com

pompom02249

Printed and bound in China.
970

Table of Contents

Safety Note:
Never point your flyer at anyone. Please ask an adult for help when making your pom-pom flyer.

Getting Started

Push something. It moves
away. Pull something. It moves
closer. Make a pom-pom flyer
that pushes and pulls.
Then watch the action!

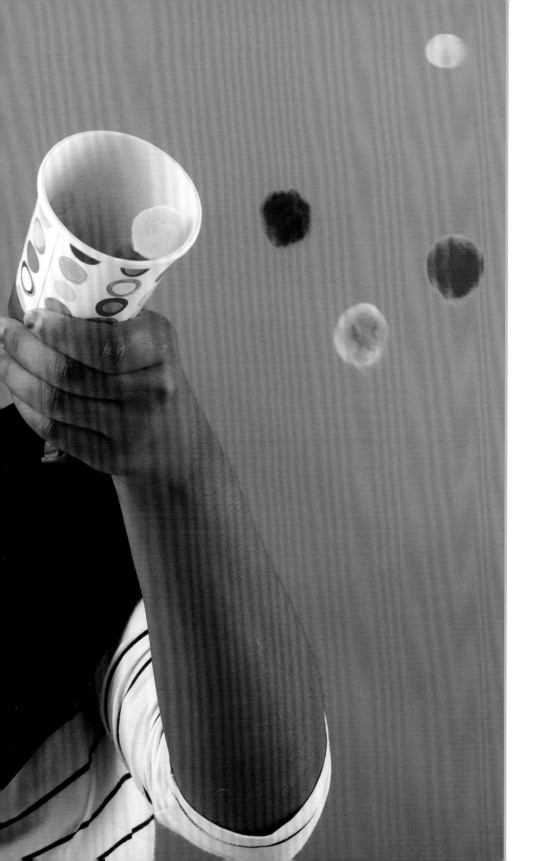

Here's what you need:

big balloon

scissors

large paper or plastic cup

pom-poms

tape measure

mini marshmallows

large marshmallows

5

Making a Pom-Pom Flyer

Tie a knot in the end
of the balloon. Then cut
a thin piece off the top
of the balloon.

Cut out the bottom of the cup.

Stretch the cut end of the balloon over the cup bottom.

Put a pom-pom into the cup. Pull the balloon knot all the way back. Stretch it as far as you can!

Now let it go! How far did
the pom-pom fly?
Measure with a tape measure
and see.

13

Try a mini marshmallow or a few.
Now try a large marshmallow.
Which flies farther? Why?

Think about the size and
weight of what's flying.

How Does It Work?

Forces make things move.
You use force when you push
or pull. You used a balloon to push
and pull. You moved pom-poms
and marshmallows with force.

Push

Pull

A balloon stretches when you pull it.

It pushes when you let go.

It pushes back with force.

Force made the pom-poms fly!

Light objects fly far. Heavier objects take more force to fly far. Pom-poms fly farther than large marshmallows. What else could you send through the air?

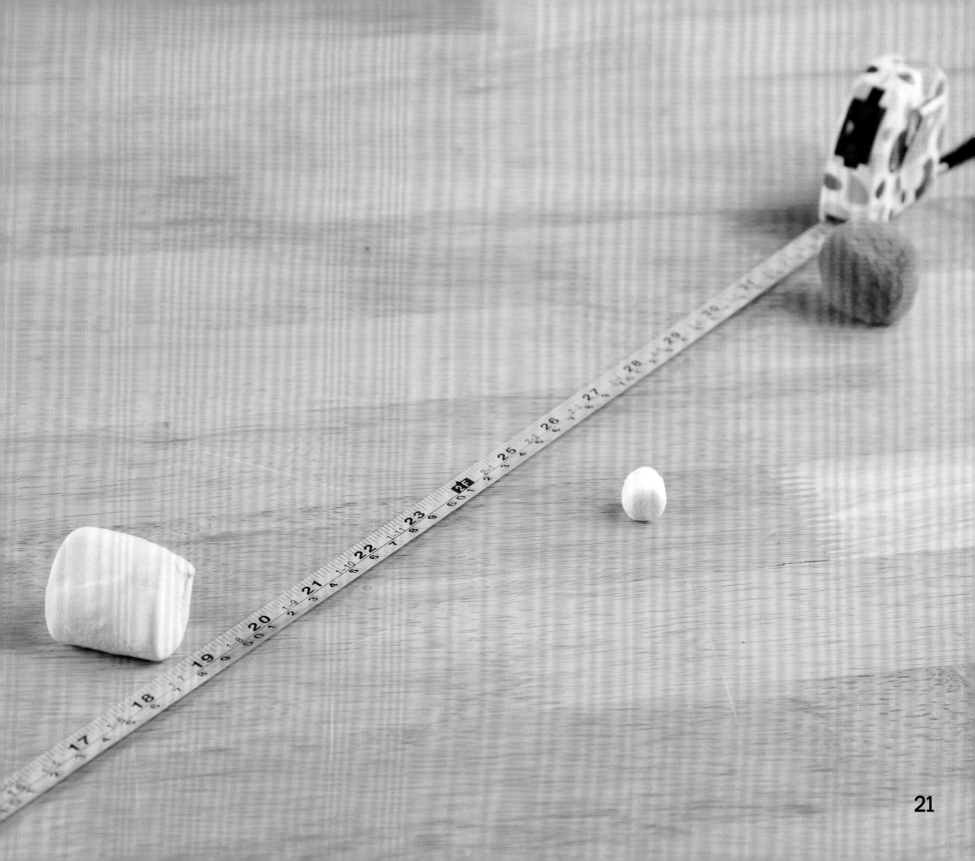

Glossary

balloon—a colorful bag of thin rubber that can be filled with air

force—energy or strength

marshmallow—a candy made of sugar and gelatin

pom-pom—a small ball of fabric or tinsel that is used for crafts

stretch—to make something longer without tearing or breaking it

Read More

Dunne, Abbie. *Forces.* Physical Science. North Mankato, Minn.: Capstone Press, 2017.

Ives, Rob. *Fun Experiments with Forces and Motion.* Amazing Science Experiments. Minneapolis: Hungry Tomato, 2018.

Weakland, Mark. *Fred Flintstone's Adventures with Pulleys: Work Smarter, Not Harder.* North Mankato, Minn.: Capstone, 2016.

Internet Sites

Use FactHound to find Internet sites related to this book.

Visit *www.facthound.com*

Just type 9781977102249 and go.

Check out projects, games and lots more at
www.capstonekids.com

Critical Thinking Questions

1. Why does a pom-pom fly differently than a marshmallow?

2. What could you do in this activity to change the distance something flies?

3. Which do you think is the more important part of this experiment—the push or the pull? Why?

Index